D1621324

Published 2023.
Little Brother Books Ltd, Ground Floor, 23 Southernhay East, Exeter, Devon, EX1 1QL
Printed in China. EU address: Korte Leemstraat 3, 2018 Antwerpen, Belgium
books@littlebrotherbooks.co.uk
www.littlebrotherbooks.co.uk
The Little Brother Books trademarks, logos, email, website addresses and the GamesWarrior logo and imprint are sole and exclusive properties of Little Brother Books Limited.

# Do you have

## WIN!

One of the coolest things about Fortnite is that you can go wild with how your avatar looks! With super skins, banging back bling and wacky weapon wraps, you can always find a way to create a unique look!

Simply send us a sceenshot of your avatar, and the GamesWarrior team will pick their 20 favourite avatar's to feature in a future GamesWarrior title. So, let's see how cool or wild your avatar's are!

## 20 WINNERS WILL GET...

**their avatar published in a future GamesWarrior title!**

## PLUS

**an advanced copy of the GamesWarrior title with their avatar inside.**

## HOW TO ENTER

### STEP 1
Take a screenshot of your avatar.

### STEP 2
Send your screenshot to competitions@littlebrotherbooks.co.uk by the 31st March 2024.

Use 'Fortnite 2024 Edition Competition' as the subject of the email.

Include your name, age, postal address and contact email address.

You must ask your parent or guardian's permission to enter the competition.

# the best avatar?

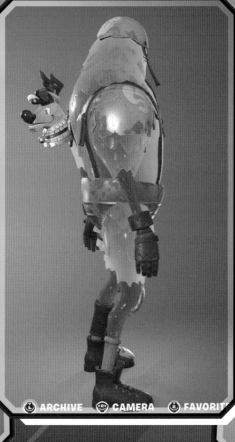

⏺ ARCHIVE ⏺ CAMERA ⏺ FAVORIT

## COMPETITION TERMS & CONDITIONS

# Fortnite
## the story explained!

There's a lot to unpack in Fortnite, especially if you are new to the world of Jonesy, The Seven and the IO. We explain some of the backstory, some of the major elements of the game, and the story of Chapter Four so far...

### In the beginning

The story behind the creation of the Fortnite universe might sound familiar. In the beginning, there was nothing. Zero. Nil. Nada. Then, in gaming's equivalent of the Big Bang, the Zero Point burst into existence. A pulsating flashing blue orb of pure energy, the Zero Point is the source of all realities. Think of it as a central point for countless multiverses, each one weirder and more wonderful than the last. The source of unimaginable power, anyone able to control the Zero Point would be able to do anything they dreamed of...

### The Imagined Order explained

The Imagined Order (IO) in Fortnite is a secretive organisation that plays a central role in the game's lore. Acting as a counterforce against the alien invasion, the IO comprises of a diverse group of agents dedicated to preserving reality and combating extraterrestrial threats. Led by the enigmatic Director, their headquarters, known as Cornucopia, houses advanced technology and serves as a hub for strategic operations. IO agents, such as Jonesy and Dr. Sloan, undertake daring missions, harnessing their unique abilities and weaponry. With their efforts, the IO strives to maintain balance and protect the Fortnite island from the encroaching otherworldly forces.

# FORTNITE BATTLE ROYALE CHAPTER 4

## Chapter Four

Over the first three chapters, the Zero Point was at the heart of ongoing battles between The Seven and the Imagined Order. The power of the Zero Point means protagonists were drawn in from all manner of multiverses – Batman, Predator, Thor, Neymar and countless others are all involved at some point. However, as we approached Chapter Four, the future of the Zero Point was as eagerly battled over as it ever was.

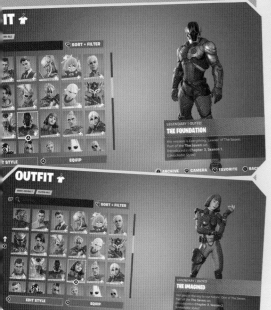

## The Seven explained

The Seven is a mysterious group in the Fortnite universe, consisting of seven enigmatic characters from different dimensions. They possess incredible powers and a deep connection to the multiverse. Originally drawn to the Fortnite island by the mysterious "Visitor," the Seven's purpose remains shrouded in secrecy. They have been involved in pivotal events, such as the Unvaulting and the Zero Crisis, reshaping the island's reality. Each member of the Seven, represented by distinct symbols, brings their unique abilities and perspectives to the table.

# Chapter Four: Season One

The most recent chapter in our amazing Fortnite adventure began with the creation of a new island, pulled together from lots of other universes. This time round, many of the buildings and areas pulled in had a medieval feel, being taken from land owned in another reality by The Oathbound. Although they seem quite primitive, The Oathbound are advanced enough to harness a material called kinetic ore which they use as a source of power.

Their headquarters is the Citadel, a large castle structure with a maze of rooms, split over many different levels. Nearby is the centre of their mining operations, a quarry by the name of Shattered Slabs. When the kinetic ore is refined, it becomes a powerful energy source that they use to make their weapons and power their vehicles. It's a completely new material to The Island and promises great power to those who wield it – which is why many characters on The Island are quick to swear allegiance to The Oathbound.

One of their number, Rift Warden Stellan, has been given the task of creating a Rift Gate, a bridge that will enable The Oathbound to travel across different realities. As well as his orders from The Oathbound, Rift Warden Stellan's dreams are haunted by an apparition that tells him of a world of perfect order, warning him of disastrous consequences if the Rift Gate is not finished.

The Scientist's Artificial Intelligence machine begins to send test subjects through test rifts, but the experience is not the smoothest. They encounter The Nothing, an evil void with malevolent intentions that changes The Scientist and the rest of The Seven into alternate versions. No-one knows what happened to their original forms.

A plan is hatched to rescue The Scientist, and the Artificial Intelligence machine begins working on a way to use Stellan's Rift Gate to bring him back. Using kinetic ore, Stellan manages to open the Rift Gate only to find that someone has sabotaged the gate, meaning it explodes, tearing the sky in two. A transmission from the Peace Syndicate then reaches The Island, with the message that 'it's time for us to come to you.'

## The Oathbound

The Oathbound is an empire shrouded in secrecy, founded by Geno and later ruled by The Ageless. They're actually predecessors of the Imagined Order who were pulled into The Island by the Zero Point. They are led by The Ageless, a young snapshot of Geno.

# Chapter Four: Season Two

As a contrast to the ancient looking structures of The Oathbound, an urban metropolis smashes into The Island at the start of Chapter Four Season Two. MEGA City looks like a cross between Blade Runner and the centre of Tokyo, with neon lights and holographic projections everywhere. It brings with it some Japanese-style technology, with amazing bikes and drift cars – all in beautiful neon colours, of course – as well as grind rails that enable the citizens of MEGA City – or anyone passing through – to grind around the place at speed.

There's even a racecourse on the outskirts – ideal for mastering those drifting skills around its many twists and turns!

Our character joins the Peace Syndicate and is asked to find whoever sabotaged the Rift Gate. It appears at first glance that whoever has done it is trying to start a war between the syndicates by causing damage to the Peace Syndicate and making it look like the other syndicates are to blame.

While checking the Peace Syndicate computers, we encounter a guy called Triarch Nox who is looking very suspicious indeed. He advises staying away from the computers – well, he would, wouldn't he? On inspection, the files on the Army of The Last Reality have been corrupted and Triarch Nox attacks (but fails!)

The unstable island is not holding up too well, however. Huge cracks begin to appear, all appearing to start from the MEGA City site. Mysterious tree roots start to creep through the gaps – it looks like there's something down there!

## The Zero Point explained

The Zero Point is a powerful energy source at the heart of the Fortnite island, possessing immense cosmic energy. It is a focal point of the game's storyline, often attracting the attention of various factions. The Zero Point has the ability to manipulate reality and has been a catalyst for significant events, causing rifts, time distortions, and even bringing about the formation of alternate realities. The battle to control the Zero Point has been a driving force behind conflicts, with characters like Agent Jonesy and the Seven seeking to harness or stabilise its power.

## The Nothing explained

In Fortnite, The Nothing is a mysterious and ominous force that threatens to consume everything in its path. It manifests as a dark void, devoid of any form or substance. Its origins and purpose remain largely unknown, but its presence poses a grave danger to the island. The Nothing consumes and erases objects, structures, and even characters from existence, leaving behind an eerie void. It serves as a constant reminder of the fragility of reality and the ongoing struggle to protect the Fortnite island.

## Agent Jones explained

Agent Jones is a pivotal character in the Fortnite storyline. Initially introduced as a member of the Imagined Order (IO), Jonesy plays a crucial role in maintaining the island's stability. However his story takes a fascinating turn. Tasked with maintaining the loop and preventing reality from collapsing, Agent Jones starts to question his purpose and becomes determined to break free from the never-ending cycle. Through encounters with characters like the Seven, his journey becomes intertwined with unraveling the mysteries of the island and finding a way to restore balance. Agent Jones embodies the struggle for liberation and brings depth to the ongoing narrative of Fortnite.

# Chapter Four: Season Three

So, Chapter Four has already seen medieval structures and futuristic neon buildings – it seems only natural that Epic throw a few dinosaurs into the mix as well! The whole central area of the map collapses, revealing an ancient jungle below.

The Zero Point is also exposed by the collapse, but it's not in a good way and looks like it is very unstable again. It transpires that Doctor Slone has been stuck in the subterranean jungle for some time, and has been studying the ruins of the civilisation that once lived there. She's recorded several audio logs with her findings and observations, and is planning to restore the buildings and civilisations to their former glory.

The Wilds, as the jungle area is known, is a lush green environment that's home to raptors that can be tamed and ridden (or raised from an egg, if you find one!). There are also vines that you can slide around on, like the grind rails from MEGA City. Coupled with the new weapons that landed at the same time, such as the Thermal DMR, and there's a whole new experience to enjoy on The Island.

The ruins in The Wilds that Sloan has been studying are overrun with greenery following centuries of neglect. Some areas even feature magic doors, where you must offer a sacrificial weapon of high standing to gain access to whatever lurks behind.

The challenge for Chapter Four Season Three then, is all about becoming king of the prehistoric jungle. Lock and load!

# Fortnite hacks

So you want to play like the pros do on YouTube? Well, aside from lots of practice, our Fortnite hacks are the fastest way to start those Victory Royales rolling in!

## Hoover up the leftovers

Always check vaults and special crates in the game, even if they have already been opened. Because they usually contain really good weapons, you'll often find whoever got there first has dropped some really useful stuff because they had the chance to upgrade on it!

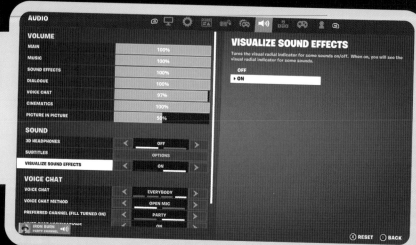

## Hide while you're vulnerable

Remember the game carries on while you're debating which augment to use, looking at the map or rearranging your inventory. If you're doing something that takes your attention from the game, make sure you take cover before doing it!

## Seeing is believing

Change your settings so that sound effects are visualised. It's far easier to see which direction gunfire and footsteps are coming from than it is to hear it!

## Out of sight

If you have to leave a particularly powerful weapon behind, don't just drop it where anyone can see it. Try and drop it in a bush, or inside a building, so that other gamers can't find it easily then use it against you!

## Don't leave presents

Don't leave things behind that might be useful to others. If you have no need for a shield keg as you pass through the area, open it and drop it so it is useless to others. Light campfires if you have enough wood, smash chug splashes even if your shield is at 100 – leave nothing behind!

## Prepare for your exit

When getting into a car, remember to equip a weapon (ideally a shotgun) first. You can't change while you're driving, and if you had your harvesting tool or a healing item in your hand when you got in, that's what you'll be holding when you get out. If there's an enemy nearby, you'll seriously regret your lack of foresight!

## Bounty hunter

Always take on a bounty if you get the chance – it costs you nothing, you'll earn gold even if someone else eliminates your target, and it can show you the position of at least one other player on the map for a while. It can be a huge help in later storm circles.

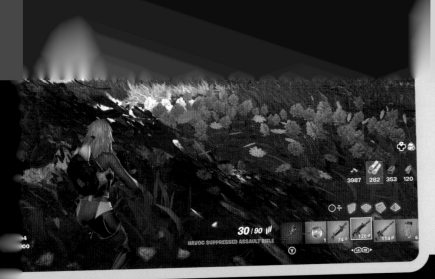

## Third party wins

Listen out for other players involved in combat with each other. Sit at a safe distance and watch, then move in to fight the winner before they can heal up, giving yourself a cheeky advantage in the process!

## Live off the land

Don't forget that there are often things around you that you can use in an emergency. Fruit, veg and mushrooms are all valuable heals when you're running low – sadly they don't count as one of your five a day though!

## Glide responsibly

The customisable features in Fortnite are all cosmetic – they don't boost your skills or stats in any way. That said, they can make a difference. When choosing your glider, it's worth considering how easily you can see where you are going – some of the bigger gliders can obscure your view which means you might land right on top of an armed opponent. Choose wisely!

## Play it safe

Any chance you have to boost your supply of gold should be taken! Look out for ways to increase your earnings by taking gold from fallen opponents, vaults, cash registers, and even by cracking safes!

# jump down stairs

To take opponents by surprise, jump down stairwells backwards so you land facing any opponents in the room below. Rather than walking down the flight you can see, spin and drop onto the other, lower flight of stairs. It can give you the element of surprise!

# i want it all!

When you first land, don't be fussy! Pick up all the weapons you find until your inventory is full and only then start to leave things behind. You'll kick yourself if you leave a weapon behind that you had space for, only for someone else to pick it up straight afterwards and eliminate you!

# Break it open!

If you're in a rush to open slurp barrels, then you don't have to break each one in turn with your harvesting tool. Standing next to them and building a small pyramid will break them immediately and you'll get that slurpy goodness immediately. This works for single barrels but is even better when there are three or four together as it saves loads of time during which you'd be vulnerable otherwise!

# Look for clues

As you approach an area, look out for signs that there might be others around. Burning campfires, opened chests, doors left open – these are all clues that you may not be alone. Knowing when to approach a building carefully can stop you being caught out by a camping opponent!

# Manage your inventory

It makes sense to keep equipment in the same slots in your inventory in each game – for example, a shotgun in slot one, an assault rifle in slot two and a sniper rifle in slot three. You'll quickly find it becomes second nature to switch between them because you just know where each weapon is when you need it, instead of having to look down at your inventory. You can set this up in the settings to make it even easier, so items are automatically assigned to the same slots each time you play!

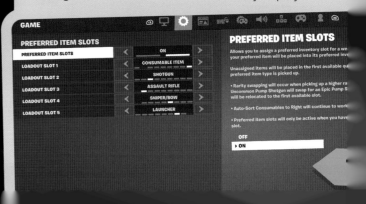

# i have the high ground

It's far easier to get shots in on your opponent if you have the higher ground, so look to take a higher route when you can. That way, if you do run into trouble you'll have a better angle to get your shots away!

# Teamwork makes the dream work

Another easy way to boost XP is to play in squads – you'll often gain the XP when one of your teammates completes a challenge. That gives you four times as many chances of completing a challenge and grabbing some extra XP into the bargain. Nice!

# All about the XP

Look for easy opportunities to boost your XP so you progress through the Battle Pass quicker. Look out for easy daily challenges, and make the most of any XP boost sessions you're given. If you know you'll be taking a break for a couple of days, line up challenges so they are NEARLY complete (for example, only needing to thank the bus driver once more) then finishing the challenges off when you are on double points for it!

# Reload

Remember to constantly check that all your weapons are fully loaded – it's the easiest thing to forget! After a battle with another player, cycle through all your weapons to check that they are all at full capacity. There's nothing worse than running out of ammo after a couple of shots and paying the price!

# Quick grab

If you encounter a chest or ammo box resting on a wooden bench or crate, it can often be quicker to use your harvesting tool to destroy whatever is beneath it than it is to open the item yourself. It means you get all the goodies, but you aren't vulnerable to a sniper for as long.

# Walk do not run

Unless you're crossing an open space, you should always move in a crouch – especially inside. You make no sound this way, which makes it much easier to surprise opponents who are running round without a care in the world.

# Harvest wisely

When gathering resources, be smart about where you get them from. Wood that's already been cut into piles usually offers a good return, for example, while wooden fences etc tend to offer a lot less return for your time. Ideally, do your harvesting early on so that you have good supply levels

– later on with a smaller storm circle, there's more chance of you running into trouble while harvesting.

# Juggling items through the storm

Sometimes you might want to carry an extra item through the storm, to use afterwards – for example, a medspray to use in the storm, as well as shield potions to keep in your inventory for any upcoming battles. Don't forget then, that you can throw consumables. Throwing medical supplies while using others on your way through the storm is perfectly possible in low tick storms, so don't feel like you have to lose consumable items just because you're in a storm – throw them, run to their new location, throw them again.

# Zip it!

When using a zipwire, you're a sitting duck to anyone looking on in a straight line. Make their life harder (and yours safer) by constantly jumping on and off the zipwire as you travel so you present a moving target!

# All in perspective

Fortnite is played in third person, so the camera is behind you. Use that to your advantage and use it to look round the edges of cover without revealing yourself as a potential target to opponents!

# Managing augments

The augment system was introduced for Chapter 4, and it allows you to gain specific powers that can help you as you battle for that Victory Royale. Choosing augments wisely is important, however – so we've put some tips together to help!

## Match with your loadout

Some augments allow you to carry extra ammo in certain types of guns, or reload quicker, for example. Match your choices to what you are carrying at the time. There's no point in selecting an augment that grants a bigger magazine for pistols when you aren't carrying one and it's late in the game. Look at what you have and try to match weapon augmentations to the weapons at your disposal!

## Spreading augments

It's often useful to make sure you have at least three of the four different augment groups covered. Choose wisely – for example there's really no point in choosing three augments that all give you heal options – just one will do, and you can use the others for different things, such as gaining ammo or accessing weapons.

# Complementary augments

Sometimes you can use augments to work in sequence so that you get a bigger advantage. For example, if you have one augment that grants you an automatic rifle, then another that increases its magazine size, then ANOTHER that speeds up reloading it – well, that just became a very powerful weapon!

# Work as a team

When you're not playing solo, it's important to talk to the rest of your squad about what augments you select! There's no point in all of you having the same augments – it makes far more sense to make sure you have all bases covered instead!

# Take cover!

Deciding on the right augment can sometimes take a few moments of thought, as you never know which two you'll be choosing between. If that's the case, make sure you take cover while you do so!

# Rerolling

You get one reroll free, meaning you can bin both the augments you've been offered and choose between two different options. Try to avoid rerolling too often outside of your free one. It costs 100 gold bars each time, and it's easy to have eaten into your savings without really realising it! Worst of all, there's no guarantee you'll get something more useful on your reroll – it could still be a choice between two unappealing options!

# Pass it on!

If you're playing in duos, trios or squads, the upgrades you can apply to weapons will stay with the weapon even after you drop it. So, if you can increase the size of an assault rifle's magazine through an augment, you can pick up a team-mate's weapon, reload it for a bigger capacity, then drop it for them to make the most of it!

# Remember what you've got!

Augments can really change the way you play, and in the middle of a long gaming session, it's easy to forget which augments you actually have. There's nothing more annoying than plunging to your doom because you had an aerialist to deploy your glider in the LAST game you played but not the one you are currently playing! It's a good idea to remind yourself of your existing augments every time you earn a new one to avoid disaster!

# Don't leave things!

If you're given two options and don't especially like either of them, choose one that won't leave a weapon behind! For example, if you have a choice between a chug cannon or faster reloading for a gun you don't have and wouldn't use anyway, select the faster reloading. Both are useless to you, but the discarded chug cannon could be picked up by a rival player and be just what they were looking for!

# Check before you upgrade

You get new augments roughly every two and a half minutes, up to a maximum of four. If you're close to getting a chance to roll for a new augment, it can be worth holding off using an upgrade bench or using keys in a holo-chest until you know what goodies the augment will bring. It might mean you keep a weapon you would otherwise ditch, or change your decision about what you'll upgrade.

# Keep up to date

Like the weapons in Fortnite, the selection of augments available changes, as new ones are introduced and existing ones are vaulted (or unvaulted). Make sure you know what the available options are so that you can play accordingly — it might make the difference between selecting a primary weapon with light ammo or medium ammo, for example.

# Don't forget your augments!

Keep an eye out for new augments arriving — you'll get a message on your HUD to tell you. Sometimes you can't access it immediately (if you're gliding or driving a vehicle for example) but don't forget to access the augment as soon as you can afterwards.

# Top classic Fortnite skins!

Although Fortnite has always been very happy to embrace other brands and franchises for inspiration, let's not forget that Epic has created some truly amazing and memorable characters all of its own too! Here's a look at some of the best Fortnite skins that you won't find anywhere else!

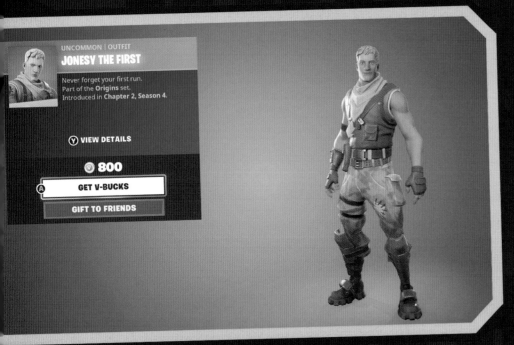

## Jonesy the first

**TYPE:** Uncommon

**COST:** 800 V-Bucks

Well, it can't be a classic Fortnite collection without this dude front and centre, can it? Jonesy IS Fortnite – he's gone from being a default skin (and is still available as one) to one of the most recognised characters in videogaming history! This skin gives you the chance to rock the OG Jonesy look!

## DJ Bop

**TYPE:** Legendary  **COST:** 2,000 V-Bucks

If, you like to get your groove on while running round the Island, then DJ Bop is the Fortnite icon you've been looking for! Get the party started with this party-tastic skin!

## Dominion

**TYPE:** Epic  **COST:** 1,500 V-Bucks

This diabolical and devilish demon is ready to paint the town red! If you're looking to terrify your opponents, then playing as one of Hades' minions seems like a pretty good place to start!

# Cobb TYPE: Rare

## COST: 1,200 V-Bucks

Get your corniest jokes ready, 'cause here comes Cobb! This farm-based Fortniter arrived in Chapter 2 Season 4 and quickly proved a firm favourite with gamers! Sweet (corn)!

# Beach Brutus

## TYPE: Rare COST: 1,300 V-Bucks

Even henchmen need some down time occasionally. Beach Brutus sees him ditch the suit and reach for the beachwear, though the Island doesn't really feel like the most relaxing place to take a break...

# Midsummer Midas

## TYPE: Epic COST: 1,600 V-Bucks

Midas may have the golden touch, but he also needs a bit of me time every now and then. As a fun extra, any weapons you touch in this skin turn to gold, so you can completely fool other players into thinking they are grabbing a legendary weapon!

# Tender Defender

## TYPE: Epic COST: 1,500 V-Bucks

Who are you calling chicken? This feathered Fortnite favourite prefers laying the smack down to laying eggs, and makes for a comical sight when he leaps into battle!

# Big Chuggus

## TYPE: Slurp Series COST: 1,500 V-Bucks

This slurp-powered big fella is not someone to be messed with! Dating back to the start of Chapter he's been putting people in their place all over the Island and cuts a menacing and intimidating figure

# Mecha Team Leader

## TYPE: Epic COST: 1,600 V-Bucks

An older skin dating back to the showdown at the end of Chapter 1, this skin was built by the Imagined Order and is a mashup of various other skins, including Drift, Rex, Beef Boss and Tomatohead.

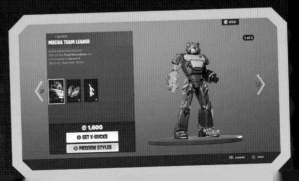

# Gaming styles

different approaches to battle your way to a Victory Royale. We've outlined some of the successful techniques used by the pros – which type of gamer are you?

## The storm chaser

**PROS:** You can be confident there is no-one behind you and the combat is all in front of you.

**CONS:** If you get delayed by combat in front of you, the storm can cause you considerable damage.

**KEY ITEM:** White heals – there's a chance you'll get caught in the storm from time to time, so your health will take the occasional hit!

This style of gameplay means you'll be keeping close to the outside of the storm circle the whole time. To begin with, you need to look for good landing sites around the edge of the map, so you know that you'll either be on the edge of the storm to start with or moving along with it as it closes.

The key thing to ensure is that the area behind you is clear, and to move only just ahead of the storm as it closes. If you do want to move to collect weapons or engage with opponents, you should be looking to move only around the edge of the storm circle, and never towards the centre. This stops anyone from getting between you and the edge of the storm.

In low tick storms, earlier on in the game, you can even move in the storm and use it as cover to pick off others! At the same time, don't always assume that there's NOTHING behind you because the storm is at your back – but if you are vigilant, staying near the edge of the storm can be an extremely effective tactic.

# The builder

**PROS:** You'll be dug into your base nice and early, and frequently will find yourself with the high ground.

**CONS:** You're making a target for yourself and may well come under attack from all sides.

**KEY ITEM:** Mats – especially brick and metal!

This style of gameplay will see you establishing yourself in a base of your own making, keeping yourself protected while picking off others as they move towards you. You'll want to drop into a fairly central area of the map to start with, so you can be confident you won't need to be moving too far. However, you'll also want to try and avoid too much combat to start with because you'll want some peace and quiet to get harvesting materials. A good technique is to land on the outskirts of a settlement to get some weapons early on, then harvest the buildings to gather metal and stone.

Once the second storm circle is revealed, head somewhere reasonably central in it, and find high ground (or an existing building). You can then construct your base, using metal and stone. You'll need to make sure you don't use ALL your mats, because the odds are you'll need to move to another location as the storm closes in – but if you are lucky and the storm seems to be centring on your current location then you can invest some more mats. Try to build more than one tower if you can, so you have different angles to shoot from, and monitor the full 360° around your build.

Weapons wise, you'll need longer-range weapons as you'll be hoping to pick people off from a distance – though a shotgun is a useful backup in case anyone does manage to get inside your build!

# The sniper

**PROS:** You can take players out from a distance before they even know you are there.

**CONS:** If someone does stumble on your location, you're in big trouble so snipers tend to have to keep moving.

**KEY ITEM:** Sniper rifle (well, duh)

Playing as a sniper is a choice that can sometimes be taken away from you if you are unlucky with the weapons you find — so it's a tactic you might have to delay until you find a sniper rifle! Once you have one, you need to be happy moving around — the sound of your rifle and the lens flare as you aim it will give your location away, so as a sniper it is about taking one or two shots, getting the elimination, then shifting to a new vantage point before you are tracked down by the other players.

A useful tip if you want to be this kind of player is that your sniper scope can now betray your position with lens flare, so don't use it all the time. Select a weapon

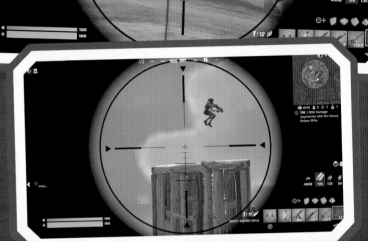

with a reasonable zoom — perhaps an assault rifle or DMR — to scan for opponents. Switch to your sniper rifle only once you've spotted one and are ready to zoom in and take the shot — it means there's less chance of you being spotted!

# The sneaker

**PROS:** It's easy to consistently make the top ten by avoiding combat.

**CONS:** You don't get much combat practice so when you do get found, you're usually toast pretty quickly!

**KEY ITEM:** Camo-style skin

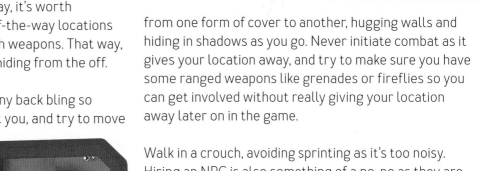

These are the players that everyone loves to hate – those that don't get involved in combat unless it's unavoidable and stay out of trouble to make the final storm circle! If you're going to play this way, it's worth investigating the map to find out-of-the-way locations to land in that are well stocked with weapons. That way, you can stock up early and go into hiding from the off.

Wear something dark and avoid shiny back bling so other players are less likely to spot you, and try to move from one form of cover to another, hugging walls and hiding in shadows as you go. Never initiate combat as it gives your location away, and try to make sure you have some ranged weapons like grenades or fireflies so you can get involved without really giving your location away later on in the game.

Walk in a crouch, avoiding sprinting as it's too noisy. Hiring an NPC is also something of a no-no as they are more visible than you and might draw unwanted attention to your location.

As you get to the final stages, try to wait until the last two players are fighting. When one is victorious, unleash everything you have at them as quickly as you can before they can heal up and reload, and you'll have a great chance of winning even though it may well be with only one elimination to your name!

# The recruiter

**PROS:** Hired help can distract rivals and eliminate opponents without you having to do a thing!

**CONS:** They can also draw attention to your location, and it's an expensive way to play the game so you might run out of gold quickly!

**KEY ITEM:** Gold bars.

Recruiters mean your plan is not to do too much of the work yourself! Learn the locations of players you can hire and head straight to them. Land on their location and hire them immediately – they'll do a great job of protecting you while you then tool up with weapons in nearby crates. Learn to work with the commands for your hireling, making sure they keep quiet when you want them to and that they are set to follow you when you move location.

Don't forget that you can also recruit animals when they are present on the island (they aren't always an option) and that boars and wolves can also be useful. Not only can they help you move around the map more quickly, they can also help you by distracting rivals in combat. However, they aren't as well behaved as hired NPCs and you can't tell them to be quiet – they just follow you around doing their thing, so they may well bring unwanted heat to your position!

# The close quarters battler

**PROS:** You can focus on specific weapons and concentrate your loadout on items that will definitely come in useful.

**CONS:** You're vulnerable if you have to cross open spaces, so you might want to pack one ranged weapon just in case.

**KEY ITEM:** Shotgun.

If you like it up close and personal, then you can focus your payload on close-range weapons – a couple of shotguns and an SMG make for a good starting point. Land in populated areas, ideally settlements with plenty of buildings that are close to the centre of the map because you don't want to be crossing open spaces too often. Load up on shotgun and SMG weapons and ammo quickly, as well as quick heals (chug splashes or

similar) because the odds are if you need to heal up, you'll be doing it with opponents nearby looking to finish you off.

Because you'll be vulnerable while crossing open ground, try to avoid moving on foot.

If you do need to move to another location, try to do so in a vehicle to minimise the risk of being engaged in a long-range sniping battle (which you'll obviously lose). This is another gaming style that lends itself well to dark clothes and no back bling as you'll be harder to see when lying in wait under staircases and in darkened corners!

# perfect backpack!

Carrying the right weapons and equipment in your back ing is essential to succeeding in Fortnite! Here is a quick guide to making the most of your loadout!

## hotguns

e right hands, a shotgun is a lethal part of your ory – but you have to use them the right way

tguns are some of the most popular weapons in nite due to their close-range lethality. They have own unique strengths and weaknesses that players understand in order to use them effectively.

ose range, shotguns can do a huge amount of damage you don't even need to be especially accurate either. shotguns have a relatively large ammo capacity and d quickly, giving you the ability to take multiple shots

However, shotguns have some notable weaknesses as wel One of the biggest is their lack of effectiveness at longer ranges. You must be extremely close in order to land shot: which can be difficult in situations where your opponents are moving quickly or using cover to stay out of range. This can make shotguns useless in open environments, where you must engage in longer-range battles.

If you're an aggressive player and like to get close to you rivals, and prefer landing and playing in urban environments rather than open areas, then you'll be wel suited to taking at least one shotgun with you!

# Pistols

The unsung hero of the game, yet one that is completely overlooked by so many Fortnite gamers! The humble pistol is useful at close range but is also surprisingly accurate at distance. Throw in a good rate of fire and quick reloads, and it makes a very solid all-round choice that can often come in handy if you decide to carry two sets of heals or explosives and want a weapon that can be useful in more than one set of circumstances.

# SMGs

SMGs, or submachine guns, are fast-firing weapons designed for close to mid-range combat.

One of their main strengths is their high rate of fire. They can quickly shred through opponents' health and shield, making them a formidable weapon in close-quarters combat. They are also relatively accurate and easy to control, allowing you to maintain your aim and accuracy even while moving at speed.

Another strength of SMGs is their versatility. They can be used in a variety of situations, from taking down opponents in tight spaces to quickly breaking down structures and cover. They are also effective at suppressing opponents, forcing them to stay in cover and limiting their ability to move and engage in combat.

However, SMGs also have some notable weaknesses. They have a limited effective range, meaning that they are not suitable for taking down opponents at a distance. This can make them less useful in open environments or in situations where opponents are using long-range weapons.

Another weakness is their limited ammo capacity. They have a relatively small magazine size and can quickly run out of ammo if not used carefully. This can make them less effective in extended battles or when facing multiple opponents.

# Sniper rifles

The absolute daddy from distance, but you need to be accurate. Long reload times mean your target may well have fled by the time you get to take a second shot, so accuracy is key. A recent change to the coding means they also give off lens flare too, so your target will see light reflecting off the scope when you have them in your sights. Coupled with the loud noise a sniper shot makes and it's easy to see why you need to get the shot right straight away – if you miss, you could find yourself being attacked in retaliation!

# Assault rifles

Assault rifles (or ARs) are the all-round kings of Fortnite weaponry. They're great for mid-range combat, and can do a job at short or long range too if you have nothing better to hand. At very close-range they can be hard to aim, but you'll rarely have to use them in such circumstances. They're pretty much the must-have weapon whenever they are available in-game, however you choose to play, because they can fit in with pretty much any type of tactic.

# Marksman rifles

The DMR rifles, like the Cobra DMR, are basically SniperLite. There's less of a drop on the bullets, the scope doesn't give off lens flare, and you can fire multiple shots without having to reload. They're pointless at close range, but if you want to be able to pick off players from distance yet lack the accuracy to make the most of a sniper rifle, these are an ideal alternative.

# Thrown explosives

Weapons you can throw at your opponents can be really handy when it comes to taking on players who are sheltering in buildings. Fireflies can even burn down wood, while grenades can knock towers down if aimed at the base. You can use them to stay hidden too, as they don't reveal where they were thrown from – it can be great to destroy players' builds as they battle each other then sweep in to pick off the victor! If you're trying to bring a build down then use explosives alongside guns to break through the structure.

# Fired explosives

Weapons like rocket launchers seem appealing, but more often than not they are pretty useless. Rockets move slowly so any kind of distance shot gives your opponents time to flee the scene, and the smoke from the rocket will also give your position away. They can be useful at fairly close range to cause huge damage to opponents, but slow reload times mean that you must get it right first time if you're using them!

# Heals

You should always save at least one slot for heals. The best ones to look for are ones that you can use quickly – those big pots look appealing with 50 shield, but it takes five seconds to sink one and you can be eliminated in that time. Chug splashes, slurp bottles, shield fish and such like are ideal because you get the goodness quicker.

Some gamers carry blue and white heals, but if you only leave one slot for heals, try to focus on heals that will repair shield or health as necessary (like chug splashes) as that way you have both bases covered!

going to affect your performance in a match or change your game play.

# Fortnite
# streamers skins

Fortnite has a HUGE online following with some streamers amassing millions of followers for their sessions on channels such as Twitch. Epic knows how important it is to get the big streamers on board, so it's no surprise that they've flattered some of them with their very own skins! Here are some of our faves – which streamer would YOU most like to play as?

## Bugha

**TYPE:** Icon Series  **COST:** 1,500 V-Bucks

Bugha (real name Kyle Giersdorf) will forever be a Fortnite legend after winning the first Fortnite World Cup – and netting a cool $3 million into the bargain!

## SypherPK

**TYPE:** Icon Series  **COST:** 1,800 V-Bucks

Sypher (Ali Hassan) has been a huge Fortnite fan since it first came out, and is still one of the most popular players to stream the game. He often brings his fans exclusive news and revelations about upcoming developments too!

## Lazarbeam

**TYPE:** Icon Series

**COST:** 1,500 V-Bucks

One of the more controversial streamers, Lazarbeam quit Twitch for YouTube in 2020 – a move that certainly worked well for the Australian streamer. His stream of 'The Device' at the end of Chapter 2 Season 2 attracted over 130,000 viewers at one point!

# achlan

**YPE:** Icon Series    **COST:** 1,500 V-Bucks

achlan Power (to give him his full name) is another
uTuber from Australia with about 17 million
bscribers! He's a pretty cool guy away from
rtnite too, and gives a lot of money to charity!

# oserfruit

**YPE:** Icon Series    **COST:** 1,500 V-Bucks

other Aussie, Loserfruit (or LuFu to her friends) moved
m League of Legends to Overwatch before seeing
uge boost in popularity when she started playing
rtnite! She's one of the most-followed female gamers,
d now has her own Fortnite skin in her honour!

# inja

**JPE:** Icon Series    **COST:** 1,500 V-Bucks

hard Tyler 'Ninja' Blevins is one of the real
tnite celebrities, with an estimated worth of $40
ion! Not surprising, given that he is the most-
owed gamer on Twitch, with over 18 million fans!

# Ali-A

**TYPE:** Icon Series    **COST:** 1,800 V-Bucks

Flying the flag for Britain, Ali-A (Alastair Aiken) is
a multi-talented gamer who is as well-known for
his Call of Duty content as his Fortnite streams.
Across all formats, he's had around nine BILLION
streams – that's amazing!

# Chica

**TYPE:** Icon Series    **COST:** 1,500 V-Bucks

Maria 'Chica' Lopez is a pro gamer who has enjoye
plenty of streaming success – as well as being the
first female member of the TSM esports team.

# The Grefg

**TYPE:** Icon Series    **COST:** 1,500 V-Bucks

David Canovas Martinez is one of Spain's biggest
YouTubers with a huge following. He revealed his
Fortnite skin on his own Twitch stream, setting a
record (at the time) with almost 2.5 million viewe

# Hired help

Often there are characters dotted around the island that you can hire in exchange for a little gold. Suddenly operating in a team of two instead of being completely alone can be a game-changer – provided you follow these golden rules!

## Master the controls

One of the more recent upgrades to the hireable NPCs is the chance to communicate directly to them so you can give them broad direction. It's only basic stuff, but you can now give them some basic orders to help them navigate the Island with you.

## Use them as a decoy

Sending your hire on a decoy mission can be a very useful way to get yourself out of a sticky situation. By ordering your hire to make a break for it in one direction, you can sometimes buy yourself enough time to sneak away undetected in the other!

# Flush out your opponents

If you have an opponent pinned down but can't flush them out of their cover, then sending in your AI teammate can work wonders. As they close in on your opponent's location they'll engage them directly or attack any builds they may have constructed.

# Follow me!

Don't forget that if you have sent your hire to a location or told them to sit still, you need to tell them to follow you again afterwards! Otherwise they'll sit where you left them and wait for the storm to finish them off without the slightest complaint!

# Res me!

If you're playing multiplayer, you can now order your hire to res(urrect) you should you get knocked. Sadly, this isn't an option in solo mode, and losing all health and shield will still result in an instant elimination.

# Shh!

One of the annoying things about the AI hires used to be that they would constantly give your position away by shooting at anything that moved, or they would just destroy whichever structure you were hiding in. You can stop that happening now, however, by ordering them to duck and be quiet. In this mode, they won't engage with anyone or anything unless they are attacked first.

# TeamWork

## makes the dream work!

Working as a team in Fortnite Battle Royale is essential to success. Here's some ways to get ahead of your rivals!

## Communication is key!

When you play with a team, you have the opportunity to communicate, coordinate your attacks, and support each other. This can be a huge advantage over teams that are not working together. Making sure your team is telling each other where they are and what they are doing is the single biggest factor in winning any of the team-based game modes — it makes you far more likely to succeed than a team that is playing as individuals. It's not just about talking either — it's about listening too, and following instructions from your team mates.

# Choose wisely

It's usually more effective (and fun) to play with people you know. Choose team mates you know and trust, and you'll soon find that working together becomes second nature. If you can play together regularly, that helps too as you will start to understand each other's style of play, strengths and weaknesses.

# Stick to the plan

While you're on Spawn Island or the Battle Bus, don't spend the time dancing or messing around. Use it to plan your game – where you'll land and what the initial strategy will be. With up to four players involved, it often becomes easier to drop in the same three or four locations so that you become well drilled in who takes which building, for example, and you are more likely to get off to a strong start.

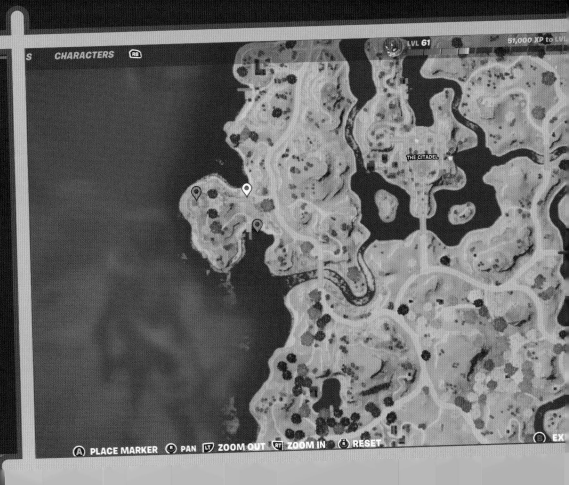

# Co-ordinate to dominate!

If you co-ordinate your attacks, you'll find things far easier. Don't go rogue, rushing into combat alone – a duo, trio or squad working together will finish you easily. Instead, you need to communicate your plan to the rest of your group, get into positions, then attack at the same time! Ideally, count down so everyone knows when to open fire. It can also help if you co-ordinate weapons – for example, one of you throws grenades which signals the start, another provides sniper cover, and two others rush the building.

# Spread the load

Try to make sure you've got all eventualities covered. You probably don't ALL need a sniper rifle – but you should make sure someone has one, for example. The same goes for heals – it's silly for two players to both be carrying one Shield Potion when one of you could carry two and the other could pick up a Medkit, for example. By sharing and spreading the weapons available among the group, you're better prepared for a wide range of situations instead of having all your eggs in one basket!

# Focus your fire

Squad games are all about numbers. If you can knock an opponent it swings the odds in your favour immediately. By agreeing to all fire at the same opponent, you will knock that one (poor) guy down quickly – now you have a numerical advantage. Next you focus on the second player, and so on. This is far more effective than each taking a different opponent and can be the deciding factor in coming out of a skirmish on top.

## Dress to impress

If you can, wear the same outfits. This will confuse opponents as they won't be sure who they have managed to damage and who they haven't, and can also make them think a player has left an area when in fact they are still there. Also, there's something to be said for matching kit. Squad goals, right there.

## Healing hands

It's a team game and it's far easier to heal than to reboot. If you can, look after your fallen brethren – build around them to stop them being finished off, and heal them as soon as it's safe to do so. If you DO need to reboot, it can save time if one of you heads to the reboot van while another goes for the reboot card (if there are more than two on the team). As soon as one player picks up the reboot card, it appears in the inventory of the other so if they happen to be at the reboot van, they can reboot immediately. This can be especially useful if the storm is closing in!

SPECTATING: MANG

YOU PLACED #35

ELIMINATED BY
MANGZHEN13870 ◇ 1

WITH
COMBAT SHOTGUN
(RARE)

REPORT PLAYER

## Be patient – and practice!

Working as a team takes time and practice. Don't get discouraged if you don't win right away. Just keep practicing and you will eventually start winning more games and getting higher in the rankings.

LVL 75      63,900 XP to LVL 76

(A) PLACE MARKER    (Y) PAN  (LT) ZOOM OUT  (RT) ZOOM IN  (X) RESET      (i) EXIT

## Be ahead of the game

Laying a trap for your opponents to blunder into requires time – it's not really something that can be done on the run. That means all these tactics are best deployed if you are in a comfortable position well inside the storm circle, rather than frantically running to keep ahead of it. Make sure there is plenty of distance between you and the edge of the storm circle, and get ready to catch them by surprise!

# Caught in

A lot of the time, Fortnite is about reacting to what's going on around you – but sometimes you can plan ahead too. When you get the chance, here are some great ways to set traps for your opponents!

## Chest camping

This one relies on a combination of sound and stealth. It works best in rooms inside building that aren't especially well lit, and are home – crucially – to a chest. If it's a legendary chest then even better! Position yourself in a corner of the room with clear sight of the door (which you should make sure is closed) and the unopened chest, then crouch down and wait. Anyone passing will hear the chest and hopefully feel compelled to investigate further. As soon as they open the door, you should be ready with your shogun or SMG!

## Loot baiting

This is a very obvious technique, but one that can be hugely rewarding. Find an area with some scattered goodies – either from chests or downed opponents – and take up a concealed position nearby. When opponents see the loot, it's inevitable that some will want to rush over to hoover up the good stuff. Little do they know you'll be waiting for them!

# Explosion in waiting

This one requires a little more forward planning, and involves leaving something explosive as part of your trap. It could be any of the situations outlined in this section, but the extra step is to leave a petrol cannister or a vehicle close to exploding next to your bait or pinchpoint. Take up a position nearby (but not too near – you don't want to get caught in the explosion yourself!) and target it with a ranged weapon such as a DMR or sniper.

Wait for your target to enter the hot zone, and fire at your explosive to initiate a fireball. Don't forget that this might not be enough to eliminate your opponent, and you may need to follow up with some shots aimed directly at them.

# a trap!

## Storm pinch point

This one works best when initiated on the edge of the storm circle, to catch those running for safety. Find a pinchpoint such as a bridge, sit tight and wait. Make sure your focus is on the storm, and look out for anyone running for safety. While they are focusing on running for safety, they probably won't even see you until it's too late. What's even better is that your target will be unable to back off or take cover because they'll be taking storm damage – often leaving them with no alternative to running straight into your firing line!

## The team trap!

This requires more than one player, though it can work with a hired NPC. One of the team acts as bait to draw enemy fire, allowing the others to target the opponents who give their position away by opening fire. The player acting as bait should be carrying heals and have maxed out shields and health, as well as enough materials to throw some decent cover up, and their teammates will need to be quick to identify their targets before their own player is eliminated first!

# Top guest appearance skins!

One of the coolest things about Fortnite is how happy other franchises are for their characters to appear as skins in the game. Let's face it – if you've not had a Fortnite skin, are you even popular? Here's a look at some of the best skins that Fortnite has borrowed from other games and films – keep a look out in the Item Store for these!

## Xenomorph

**TYPE:** Epic  **COST:** 1,600 V-Bucks

The terrifying creature from the Alien franchise isn't content with terrorising Ripley from one galaxy to the next – now it's landed in Fortnite and is ready to do the same to Jonesy and co!

## Robocop

**TYPE:** Epic  **COST:** 1,500 V-Bucks

Serve the public trust. Protect the innocent. Uphold the law. Robocop landed in Fortnite all guns blazing, and is an epic skin in every sense of the word! Half man, half machine, all Fortnite!

## Harley Quinn

**TYPE:** DC Series

**COST:** 1,500 V-Bucks

Who could resist the chance to play as this iconic DC Comics character, complete with her signature pigtails, makeup, and mallet? It's a unique and playful way to show off your love for the Joker's better half.

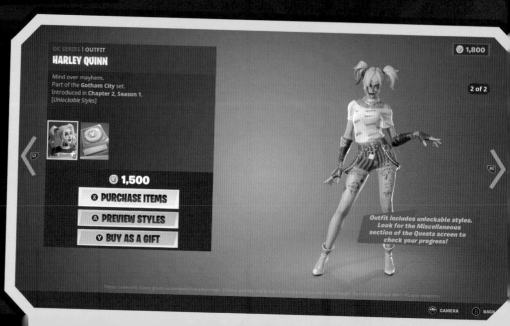

# John Wick

**TYPE:** Legendary    **COST:** 2,000 V-Bucks

In this skin, you can embody the legendary hitman and his slick, deadly style. With his black suit, tactical gear, and sleek hair, he's the ultimate badass to take on opponents in the game.

# The Flash

**TYPE:** DC Series    **COST:** 1,500 V-Bucks

...lay in the iconic bright red outfit of The Flash. ...adly, the skin doesn't allow you to zip round the ...ap in the blink of an eye — but you will look pretty ...ool wearing it, which is the most important thing!

# Blanka

**TYPE:** Gaming Legends Series

**COST:** 1,600 V-Bucks

...anka from Street Fighter is one of the most ...cognisable gaming characters in history, so ...eryone was stoked when he made it to Fortnite! ... bright green skin means your opponents will ... you coming — but will they be able to stop you?

# Master Chief

**TYPE:** Gaming Legends Series

**COST:** 1,500 V-Bucks

Even Master Chief knows that Fortnite is bette... than Halo, so it was no surprise when he finally rocked up on the Island to join the fun! His camo... outfit makes this a useful skin to employ if you don't want to be spotted!

# Catwoman

**TYPE:** DC Series    **COST:** 1,500 V-Bucks

Based on the comic books rather than the films, this classic outfit is a great choice — especially if you love to leap and climb your way to a Victory Royale! All this AND you ca... hide in the shadows! Miaow!

# Rey

**TYPE:** Star Wars Series

**COST:** 1,500 V-Bucks

From scavenging scrap metal from spaceshi... wrecks to becoming the galaxy's most powe... Jedi, Rey knows a thing or two about the lon... slog to the top. Makes her a great choice to ... that Victory Royale with then!

# Getting Around

There are lots of different types of vehicle you can use to help you get around on Fortnite Island – here are some of the pros and cons of the most popular modes of transport!

## Bikes

Motorbikes are relatively new additions, with trail bikes appearing in Chapter 4 Season 1, then Rogue bikes (souped up racers) arriving in Chapter 4 Season 3.

### Strengths

Bikes are fast and nimble, with small turning circles and able to fit through small gaps, such as down alleyways. This makes them an excellent choice if you're looking to make a quick getaway from a battle, as you can be out of sight relatively quickly and it's easy to zip in and out of cover as you put distance between you and the opponents you are fleeing from.

The speed of a bike also means you can catch some serious air, so they can be used to reach the tops of buildings or get over gaps that might otherwise cause you delays. This makes them a great choice if you're trying to get away from the storm, as they can help you get over obstacles as well as doing so at speed.

You can also cycle through your weapons while riding a bike (something you can't do when driving a car) as well as reload and use heals. What's more, you can fire your weapon from the bike, meaning it's a great option if you spot an opponent and fancy taking a couple of pot shots before getting straight outta dodge.

### Weaknesses

The obvious drawbacks to bikes are that they can only accommodate two players, so are no good if you are playing squads and you all need to move together.

Secondly – and more of a problem – is that there's no protection on a bike. If you're in a car or lorry, the chassis of the vehicle will offer a lot of protection if you are fired on. On a bike, you have no such luck and it's actually possible to be eliminated outright while on a bike, bringing a premature end to your fun.

This issue is made worse by the fact that bikes are noisy, and can be heard from a long way off. As such, it makes sense to use bikes for short sharp bursts from place to place before getting off and taking cover – then using the bike again to reach the next area you need to get to.

# Boats

Although you can swim through the rivers, lakes and seas around the Island, who wants to get their bling wet? Keep your feet dry and deal out some destruction along the way with our guide to nautical navigation!

## Strengths

The weaponry aboard a boat is extremely handy! As well as being able to fire your own weapons while steering, you also have access to rockets that can destroy builds in seconds. It does take a couple of seconds to reload, but the wait is worth it. You also have a wide shooting range, even being able to aim at targets behind you.

Boats are also very fast in the water – far faster than swimming. If you're in an open area of water, the odds are that you are visible from pretty much every angle. Even worse, your movement is pretty predictable when swimming and it's not as easy to throw up builds as quickly as it is online. Basically if you're getting wet, you're far better off in a boat!

## Weaknesses

As with bikes, there's not really a chassis between you and your opponents so you can be sniped on a boat and eliminated instantly by a crack shot. This can be a particular problem if you're in open water (though still much better than being forced to swim!) so try to avoid that risk by zigzagging constantly and always presenting a moving target!

Although boats can travel on land, it's a pointless exercise as they sustain damage as well as moving incredibly slowly. You'll be a sitting duck so get out of the boat once you run out of water. The only exception would be if you can cross a small section of land to get to another expanse of water, in which case it might be worth sticking with the boat – but it's certainly a risk!

# Airborne vehicles

In Fortnite, you can fly! Well, sometimes. Although planes and choppas are often vaulted, they can be game changers when they are available – here's how to use that to your advantage!

## Strengths

Well, the main strength of a choppa or plane is a pretty obvious one – you're in the air! This gives you a very different perspective on the madness unfolding down below – you will often be able to spot skirmishes or players running across the landscape that you'd never have a hope of spotting from ground level. You can use this to suit however you like to play – you can find a quiet landing spot away from all the action if you like to lie low, or head straight for the gunfire if you want to throw yourself into the heart of the battle from the off!

As well as giving you a fantastic view of the action, travelling by air means you can travel long distances very quickly as you can just head in a straight line. This can give you an advantage when a new storm circle is revealed, for example, as you can get into position there faster than anyone who is on the ground and needs to navigate mountains, gullies, rivers and so on.

You can also use choppas and planes to move from one area of high ground to another without ever having to surrender the advantage! You can simply fly from one mountain top to another as the storm circle changes, making sure you're always looking down on your opponents!

## Weaknesses

The flipside of being able to see the combat stretching out below you is that you're visible to pretty much everyone! That means they can shoot at you, and they'll have a heads up about the area you've landed in. To avoid being sniped or hit with rockets, try to keep moving and don't hover or fly too low to make things easy for them. As the storm circle gets smaller, staying in the air becomes less of an attractive option – it's best to move between locations while airborne rather than just staying up high for the whole game.

In choppas (and some planes) you can't shoot while piloting. That means you're defenceless against attack, unless you're playing squads and have a sniper on board to return fire. You can hop into the passenger seat to shoot, but you'll start dropping like a stone and won't be able to avoid attack, so that's not really an option.

Lastly – it's a long way down! If your aircraft takes too much damage and explodes mid-air, the fall will kill you – so if you start taking heavy damage get out of the sky as quickly as you can and revert to groundwork!

# Cars and trucks

The everyday way of zooming around the Island, cars and trucks are usually pretty easy to find – but there are still a few tricks to getting the most out of them.

## Strengths

There's nothing particularly special about most of the cars and trucks in the game, and none that make them stand out enough for them to form a key part of your strategy. However, they are all a lot faster than walking and if you like playing in built-up areas more than open space, they can get you between them quickly and with less chance of being sniped while you cross open ground.

Another advantage to cars and trucks is that they make great hiding places. Simply change seat so you're in the passenger seat and the engine will turn off, leaving you in silence. It's amazing how few players will even check to see if anyone is sitting in a car, so you can either open fire out of the window or jump out and surprise them! Alternatively, you can just sit quietly and wait until your opponent has disappeared from view!

## Weaknesses

Vehicles used to be pretty indestructible, but they were seriously nerfed during Chapter 3 and now most of them will blow up pretty quickly if fired on. They're especially vulnerable to SMGs but all weapons can cause them a lot of damage very quickly – especially in squads where a whole team can concentrate their fire on one.

To add to the problems, you can't shoot while driving, so you're especially vulnerable if you do run into gunfire. This makes trucks and cars more useful in duos, trios or squads as your teammates can fire from the vehicle, making you less of a sitting duck!

Because you can't change weapons while in a car or truck, you should always make sure you have a shotgun or SMG equipped BEFORE you get in. That way, if you have to ditch at short notice, you're ready to fight.

# Tanks and big rigs

Tanks and lorries are the big boys of the Fortnite vehicle world – and they come with their own pros and cons!

### Strengths

Driving a big boy like a tank or an artic cab means that you don't have to worry too much about going round things – you can just go through them! You can use the weight of the vehicle to break through some structures, though it will depend how quickly you are going. At a reasonable speed you'll be able to drive straight through most wooden walls etc, but if you are going slowly, don't be surprised if you find yourself coming to a standstill straight after any collision!

If you're behind the wheel of a tank, then you'll also have some pretty impressive weaponry at your disposal, including missiles that can lock onto targets. Use these to your advantage, but be aware that they take their sweet time to reload!

You'll often find a truck cab in front of a tanker of slurp juice – if you need a shield you can hop in the cab and then reverse into the tanker to quickly release the goodness!

### Weaknesses

The main issue with the bigger vehicles is that they are very slow, and you won't be outrunning anyone! Admittedly they can take more damage than smaller vehicles, but you'll still be very vulnerable if you come under fire (this is more of a problem in a lorry than a tank). If you can't return fire quickly you will find yourself with smoke pouring out of your vehicle and you'll need to evacuate fast!

Another issue caused by the sheer size of these behemoth vehicles is that they struggle with hills. If you approach a hill and don't have any momentum, you'll pretty much crawl up it very slowly. This is guaranteed to happen at the worst times, so the best approach is to keep moving when you're in a larger vehicle rather than stopping and starting all the time. Take longer, slower bends where you can to keep the speed and momentum high, rather than slowing down to make tight turns because the lack of acceleration can leave you in big trouble if an opponent shows up at that moment!

# Handheld transport

As well as the more traditional vehicles, sometimes Fortnite is home to handheld, more immediate methods of getting around! These include items like the Kinetic Blade or the Grappler Gun.

### Strengths

The great thing about these forms of transport is that they are 'on demand' – that is, you can have them in your inventory but you don't have to use them all the time. With a car, you're either in it or you're not, but with something like a Kinetic Blade, it's there when you need it the moment that you do.

That means that these weapons are the perfect solution for quick getaways from combat, or for those moments when you realise the storm is right behind you and moving quicker than you are. Simply equip your transport and zoom right out of trouble!

### Weaknesses

These items take up a space in your inventory, so you lose a space that would otherwise be home to a weapon or a heal. You need to weigh up the pros and cons of having such an item – it might even be that you dump it in the latter stages when the storm circle is small, as you are less likely to need them.

Most items of this type also have a limited number of uses before they need to be recharged, so you need to be aware of that. If you've just landed after using one,

for example, you might want to stay behind cover until it has recharged in case you come under another attack and need to move on quickly again.

The final weakness is that these weapons are quite noisy when used, so you might be drawing attention to your location when you so use them. The smaller the storm circle, the greater that risk, so you will need to expect people to come looking for you, especially once you are inside the top ten players or so.

# The Ultimate Guide to
# urban combat

If you like to do your battling in buildings, then our guide to urban combat will help you secure that elusive Victory Royale!

## Outfit

If you want to operate in the built-up areas in Fortnite, you will need to avoid being seen. Most of the buildings in Fortnite are pretty dark inside, so darker skins definitely work better when it comes to urban combat. When you find yourself in the same room as another player, every split second counts. If you're wearing something bright and make it easier for them to hit you, then that could be game over. The same goes for being spotted as you move from building to building.

For that reason, look for dark skins that match the colours of the buildings, and enable you to hide in the shadows when you need to. Outright blacks are good, as are dark greys – grey means you can hide in darkness, but can also help you blend in against walls!

## Weapons

The shotgun is definitely your friend in urban combat, and you'll probably want to carry two of those bad boys. Switching from an empty shotgun to a full one can save you time reloading and mean you aren't left defenceless in the middle of a gunfight or with your opponent closing in on your location while you hurriedly reload.

Aside from shotguns, the SMG is another excellent option – either as a third weapon or in place of your second shottie. Its quickfire nature means it is well suited to close quarters combat but it can also be useful if an opponent throws up a wall while you battle.

You might want to consider the possibility of longer range weapon such as an assault rifle to help keep you safe if you have to move from one location to the next, though this could easily be sacrificed if there are handheld transportation devices available (Kinetic Blades, Spidey's Webs etc) as it's better to be rapid between locations.

## Explosives

Explosives aren't really your friend if you like urban combat. They take a valuable space up and because you'll often be in the same building as your target, deploying grenades or fireflies will almost certainly end up causing you damage as well as your opponent. They can come in handy for clearing buildings if you know opponents have already entered them, but as a rule they shouldn't form part of your standard loadout!

## Heals

If you're involved in urban combat, you won't have the luxury of time when it comes to healing, so prioritise anything that's QUICK. Fish that can be gobbled down in a second, chug splashes, slap juices – if you can get your health or shield up fast, take it with you. Big shield potions may look attractive, but they take five seconds to down and the noise you make while healing can be enough to give you away in an urban combat environment. Don't take the risk – make sure you're well-stocked with instant heals.

## Materials

You won't be building much in urban combat, so don't worry too much about building materials. Grab what you can from chests and fallen opponents — you might find you need to throw up the occasional defensive wall in larger rooms if you're taken by surprise but for the most part you'll be using existing cover rather than building your own.

The only possible exception to that rule would be if you want to knock out a section of wall and replace it with an editable slab of your own build so you can see your opponents coming, or build ramps up to enter buildings from the top rather than the bottom. In either case, you won't be burning your way through loads of mats to achieve it, and you're actually better off avoiding drawing too much attention to yourself anyways, so harvesting is best avoided.

If you absolutely have to gather materials for any reason, it's best to do it using the internal walls in a building (rather than the outside walls, which can leave a gap you might be sniped through!)

## Drop spots

Look for built-up areas that are fairly central, because you don't want to be moving around too much once the game gets going. It's best to invest time in really learning the layout of three or four central built-up areas so that you know what to do when you land at each one — where you're likely to find chests, good hiding spots and so on.

## Movement

Your footsteps will give your position away inside buildings. Anyone above or below you will hear you very clearly, and you'll also draw the attention of anyone passing the building you're hiding in. Once you're inside an urban environment, you should stay crouched and move slowly. However, when you are outside, you're vulnerable to sniper fire so be quick as you zoom from building to building!

## High or low

Wherever you can, try to reach the higher floors in buildings. Either head up the stairs once inside, or build up and enter via the roof. If opponents find their way into your building, you want to be aiming down at them from the top of a staircase, not aiming upwards. Find the high ground inside each building you enter and make sure you stay there until it's time to leave.

## Storm management

You want to be in position early – that's why the aim is to drop fairly central so that you can get into a built-up area from the off. If things don't go your way, however, you might find yourself outside the storm circle. Should this happen, move QUICKLY to a new built-up location in the new storm circle. You want to be in position early, so that other players are moving into your building – not arriving late and getting caught in an ambush yourself. If you can, grab a vehicle or rift to get between locations as you'll be especially vulnerable while on the move. If you're left with no alternative but moving on foot, then it might be worth dumping a shotgun or SMG and picking up a sniper rifle or marksman rifle for the journey – you can always swap it back once you're in your new location.

# The ultimate guide to open combat

Come and have a go if you think you're hard enough! If you like your fighting to be loud, proud and in your face then this is the best way to go about it – but be warned, it's a high-risk policy!

## Outfit

If you're happy to be out in the middle of the conflict, you may as well go the whole hog and make a real exhibition of yourself! Playing in this way, making no attempt to stay out of sight, means you'll need to be good as well as confident. It's something to build up to, but once you feel ready, you may as well have some fun. Load up on outrageous outfits, the brighter the better. You won't be trying to hide, so you may as well stand out, after all. Luminous back bling? Crazy weapon wraps? Noisy, over-the-top gliders that can pretty much be seen from space? Say YES YES YES to all of these and more – you're playing as a show-off so why on earth not make the most of it?

## Weapons

If you're going to be relatively indiscreet when it comes to your combat, you'll find that you need to be prepared for pretty much any eventuality. Some opponents will engage you at range; others will try their best to sneak up on you and surprise you with a shotgun jabbed into your ribs. For that reason, make sure you have a good spread of weapons. This should include a shotgun as a necessity, along with a decent mid-range weapon. Ideally this should be an assault rifle, though an SMG will suffice if you can't find one early on.

To complete the set, a sniper or marksman rifle will give you the ability to pick people off from distance – an option you should be looking to take as often as you can. If you're looking to carry four weapons, then sacrifice your explosives slot and add the SMG as well as your assault rifle, meaning you'll have all bases covered pretty much.

# Explosives

Because you're not trying to avoid attention – in fact, you CRAVE attention – there's no harm in grabbing yourself a rocket launcher if such a thing is available. Maximum damage, maximum noise – what's not to love? In any case, explosives of some kind (even fireflies or grenades) will often be useful because you'll often find that your opponents will build cover while they try to launch attacks at you. No cover means a much easier job for you, and explosives can help you achieve that!

# Heals

Because you'll be a very clear presence in combat, it's inevitable that you'll take on some damage from time to time. You'll need to heal quickly, because the odds are the next attack is only seconds away, so look to prioritise quick heals, or those that allow you to keep fighting while you use them. Items such as Chug Splashes, Slap Juices or Splash Barrels are ideal – if you're using the barrels you'll need to turtle to be on the safe side but then you can edit yourself a window and get on with the combat!

# Materials

If you're playing in an open and aggressive way, it's really important that you are carrying plenty of materials. Get harvesting immediately – ideally, try to drop near a built-up area so that you have a good supply of stone and metal from the off. Wooden walls are great as a temporary measure, but if you're setting yourself up to defend a solid base you'll want it to be built of sterner stuff. Make brick your priority as it has the best balance between build speed and sturdiness, then look to add metal sections once you have the basics down.

As the game goes on, make sure you try to plunder the loot of any fallen opponents – by the fourth or fifth storm circle, most players will be carrying quite a lot of materials. Taking it from them is ideal – you don't have the time or space for extensive harvesting, but you're likely to have used a lot of your own initial supplies due to the need to defend yourself.

## Movement

Being visible and central means that everyone knows where you are, or at least where you've just been, so there's no point in creeping around. In fact, creeping around would be a really bad idea – you'll be easier to hit. Be fast, be loud, be confident! It doesn't matter who hears you coming, they won't stand a chance anyway!

## Drop spots

Choosing where to drop is pretty simple, really. Two words – go central. The aim of this gameplay style is to let others come to you, with you in a well-established base (of your own building or not). That's a waste of time and effort if you build it on the outer edges of the map and then have to abandon it without a shot being fired from it. Try to aim for areas that are also near to towns or buildings so that you can get busy building your materials from the off too – you'll need them later in the game so it makes sense to start early!

# High or low

If you're being highly visible in your approach, it's more important than ever to make the most of high ground. Make sure no-one is looking down on you, and if opponents start to build to try and make that happen, either build upwards yourself or destroy their build before they can give themselves an advantage over you!

# Storm management

You want to be in position early with others moving to you. That's why you should be landing centrally, and if the storm circle isn't favourable to you and you need to move again, do it quickly rather than holding back and letting the storm push you along – you'll be running into other players' fire, when you want it to be the other way round!

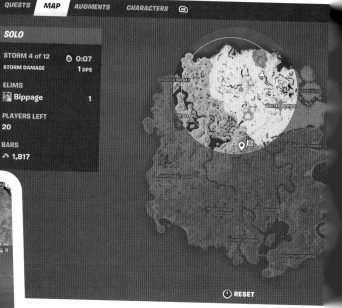

# The ultimate guide to covert combat

If hiding in shadows and bushes and keeping out of trouble appeals to you, then our guide can help you secure a Victory Royale without most of your opponents even knowing you're there!

## Outfit

If you want to play covertly, then you can't stand out from the scenery. Forget any ideas about back bling or colourful weapon wraps — you want to be at one with nature and that means keeping everything green (perhaps brown or black at a push!)

Wherever possible, you should be looking to get yourself into a bush or pile of leaves, but sometimes you'll need to hide behind cover — a boulder, for example, or pressed flat against a canyon wall. To avoid being spotted, it makes most sense to opt for dark, muted skins that are largely one colour, rather than being drawn to anything bright and contrasting.

## Weapons

The key to covert combat is to avoid detection as much as possible, so if there are any silenced or suppressed weapons available in the game, you should definitely be looking to add them to your payload. Aside from that, you need to focus more on taking out opponents from a distance rather than getting into close quarters combat, so look for marksman rifles or sniper rifles whenever possible. These will enable you to hit opponents from a distance while you are safely in cover, minimising the risks of being seen while you do it.

However, you will also need to have a shotgun available should anyone blunder into your bush or manage to get close to you. If you only have long and mid-range weapons available, you won't stand a chance up close and even though it's not part of the plan, it's best to be prepared should you need to engage in close quarters combat at any point.

# Explosives

Because your primary focus should always be to not give your location away too easily, fired explosives (such as rocket launchers) are not something you should consider using. The vapour train and noise they make will make it really obvious to anyone within earshot exactly where they can find you.

Thrown explosives, however, can be a very useful addition to your armoury. Firefly jars or grenades won't give you away, because they only really make noise when they land – and they could have come from anywhere. Admittedly an eagle eyed opponent might spot where they came from, but it's highly unlikely – so you can use them to your advantage to help take down builds or even go for outright eliminations with them!

# Heals

Because you'll be keeping your distance from other players, you don't need to worry too much about being heard while you heal up – and because you'll be out of sight most of the time, you won't be vulnerable while you heal up either. To make the most of this, you should prioritise bigger healing items such as full Medkits or large Shield Potions because you'll have the time to take them. If you're happy carrying two heal slots then take both, but if you need to choose one, go for Shield Potions over Medkits.

# Materials

You won't be building too much when playing covertly, as a building going up will bring you unwanted attention. That said, you'll need to have some materials to hand should you need to build up to higher ground, or as landing platforms while you head down sheer drops. It might also be necessary to throw a few defensive walls up at short notice should you come under fire, so you'll need to be carrying something to help do that.

The best approach is therefore to harvest some materials quickly – wood is fine – at the start of the game where there's less chance of you being heard or seen while doing it. Aside from that, you can rely on keeping whatever you plunder from your victims or find on your travels around the Island.

# Drop spots

Choosing where to land as a covert player is actually open – you can look to land on the outside of the map to keep the storm at your back, or land centrally so that you don't have to move too much once you're settled into your hiding spot. In either case, you need to do some research into out-of-the-way landing spots that are home to decent amounts of loot but won't involve an all-out fight from the second your boots hit the ground.

# Movement

The whole point of covert combat is to keep movement to a minimum and not draw attention to yourself or your position if you can avoid it at all. For that reason, it's best to avoid movement as much as possible – find a bush or vantage point, crouch down and stay out of sight. If you do have to move, remember that your opponents are more likely to spot movement if you are running, so try to stay crouched and sneak around. That also means you're less likely to be heard by anyone who is nearby too. You should be looking to move from one form of cover to another, avoiding long periods of being out in the open.

# High or low

High ground is always better for sniping and shooting, but when you're hiding, there's a lot to be said for staying low. Canyons and gullies can often offer extra cover and more shadows, and players are less likely to head for low ground so sometimes it's an easier way to stay out of trouble. Your main focus should be the quality of the cover, and not worrying too much about high ground until the last couple of storm circles when the numbers are smaller and you'll need that high ground advantage.

# Storm management

You can be quite flexible in your approach when playing covertly. Some players prefer to land in the middle of the map, load up with weapons and then head to a hiding spot that they won't have to leave for quite a while.

Others prefer to land on the edges of the map and move with the storm at the back, safe in the knowledge that the battle is unfolding in front of them so there is little chance of being ambushed from behind.

Both are perfectly sensible ways to play, so go with whichever one suits you best – or chop and change depending on the Battle Bus route! In any case, if you do have to move to stay in the storm, try to leave it late so that you are less likely to be spotted – most players are looking into the centre rather than out at the edges, and you can form your plan as you approach the new storm circle.

# Top bargain skins!

You don't need to break the bank in order to look good in Fortnite! While some skins can cost up to 2,000 V-Bucks, there are plenty of cheaper alternatives. Check out our list of bargains – they all look fantastic, and they're all priced at just 800 V-Bucks!

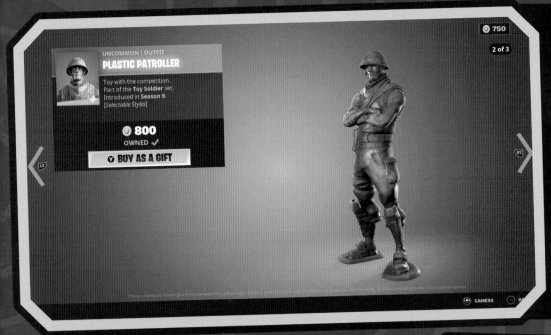

## Plastic Patroller

**TYPE:** Uncommon

**COST:** 800 V-Bucks

One of the best skins in the game, and happily also one of the cheapest! Plastic Patroller is a perfect match for most of the greenery in the game, helping you to stay out of sight of your opponents as well as coming in at the lowest price point. Sweet!

## BRUTE Gunner

**TYPE:** Uncommon **COST:** 800 V-Bucks

This skin exudes intimidation and power. Its bulky armour and helmet make it a formidable choice if you are the type of player who likes to show dominance on the battlefield!

## 501st Trooper

**TYPE:** Star Wars Series **COST:** 800 V-Bucks

If you're after a Star Wars skin, this is definitely the best value for money option out there! 501st Trooper tends to pop up most times there are Star Wars tie-ins, so if you cant stretch to a Darth Vader or a Rey, this guy can still make sure you get your Star Wars fix!

# Birdie

**TYPE:** Uncommon **COST:** 800 V-Bucks

Fore! If you like a sporty look, then Birdie might just be the hole in one you're looking for! The bright colours will make you stand out, but that just makes it all the more fun!

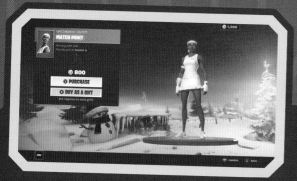

# Match Point

**TYPE:** Uncommon **COST:** 800 V-Bucks

Another sports-inspired skin, Match Point is an outfit worth making a racket about! This ace skin might help you lay a grand slam down on your opponents, bringing that Victory Royale within your grasp. The ball's in your court!

# Hayseed

**TYPE:** Uncommon **COST:** 800 V-Bucks

He might look like something of a country bumpkin, but Hayseed is a Fortnite veteran and often pops up as an NPC. That makes this skin a great option if you want to lay a trap for others, waiting until they approach you before revealing you're not an NPC at all!

# Crustina

**TYPE:** Uncommon **COST:** 800 V-Bucks

One of the fast food favourites from Fortnite, Crustina is a pizza perfection. With a tomato for a head, you need to make sure no-one turns you into ketchup though! Like your local pizza place, this outfit always delivers.

# Scout

**TYPE:** Uncommon **COST:** 800 V-Bucks

Poor old Scout is another OG skin but one that gets next to no attention compared to Jonesy! You can change that though, and give this skin the love it deserves, helping Scout to the top of the pile!

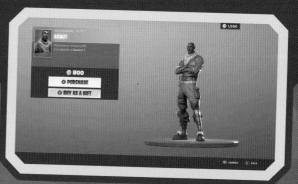

# Whistle Warrior

**TYPE:** Uncommon **COST:** 800 V-Bucks

When it comes to authority figures, few strike as much fear into people as the sight of a referee! Get your whistle at the ready and be prepared to put your opponents firmly in their place with this striped skin!

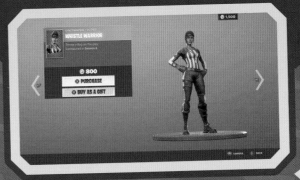

# Building Guide

Building is an essential part of Fortnite, and you'll need to master the basics at the very least!

## Use the right materials

There are three types of materials you can build with: wood, stone, and metal. Wood is the quickest to build with, but it is also the weakest. Stone is more durable than wood, but takes longer to build, while metal can sustain the most damage but takes the longest.

In general, you should use wood for quick builds and stone or metal for more permanent structures. If you suddenly come under fire while crossing a field, for example, a quick wooden wall between you and the gunfire can help buy you valuable seconds. If you're looking to build a structure to snipe from and expect it to come under attack from other players, then you should be using stone or metal however – not only can they take more damage, they won't catch fire if your opponents have any weapons that involve flames!

# Practice makes perfect

It's a cliché, but it's true. You need to practice your building constantly, in creative modes or building-based games as well as in Battle Royale mode. The more you build, the more it will become second nature to you – especially repetitive tasks such as building a hut to heal in, throwing up a wall as a shield, or the all-important art of cranking 90s.

# Learn how to edit

Editing is a very important part of building. It allows you to change the shape of your structures, which can give you an advantage in battle. For example, you can edit a wall to create a window, which you can shoot out of at enemies. If you get really fast, you can edit a window, take a shot, then edit to remove the window before your target can return fire!

# Build on what's there

Adding to an existing building can save you time and materials, so look out for suitable structures that are in good locations. Adding turrets, towers and walkways to them is a great way to acquire an impressive base very quickly. You can also amend the existing building – for example, destroying a solid wall and building your own in its place, then editing a window in for improved coverage.

# Cuckoo!

You don't always have to do the building yourself! Sometimes you'll find a player-built structure that's been abandoned and you can pop into it and make it your own. Sometimes, other gamers will have seen the other player leave the base (or be shot in it) and if you're sneaky they'll assume it's empty which can give you a headstart on them!

You can then add a few little touches of your own, and perhaps replace a few existing parts of the structures with ones of your own so you can edit them, and you're good to go!

# Cranking 90s

Cranking 90s is a building technique that allows you to quickly gain height. It is a very important skill to learn if you want to be successful in the game.

To crank 90s, you will need to place a ramp, a wall, and a floor in quick succession. You will also need to rotate your character 90 degrees each time you place a build.

The first step is to place three walls forming three sides of a box. You can then place a ramp and run to the top of it, sticking to either the left or right-hand side. At the top of the ramp, turn to face inwards towards the box (so, if you ran up the left side of the ramp, turn right). Now repeat the process – three walls and a ramp. You can keep doing this over and over until you reach the desired height, sniping from the top or reaching higher ground once you get there.

Be careful not to go too high, however – the bottom of your tower can easily be destroyed leaving you to plunge to your doom!

# Turtling

Turtling is a defensive strategy where players build a 1x1 box around themselves to protect themselves from enemy fire. It can be effective, but needs to be used in the right situations to avoid being destroyed too easily.

If you're turtling while you heal up, then it's okay to use wood but if you're turtling while in combat, then use stone or metal. Don't forget to add a roof, and be quick to edit a window so that you can fire at your opponent. Try to make sure the rear of your hut is against a wall or cliff so that no-one sneaks up behind you during your battle.

Once you've built your hut and edited your window in, it's important to be quick getting your shots away. If you stand still, framed by the window – well, there's no point in having cover to start with. Use the wall to shield yourself, step into the window to take your shot, then edit the window back out or move away from it quickly!

Don't make turtling your first option in combat. You should only really do it if you are badly wounded and need to heal, and there's no other easy way to escape from the situation. Build quickly, heal up, win the battle and move on!

# Mix it up!

There's so much more to Fortnite than Battle Royale. There are plenty of official and unofficial alternative game modes available – here is a selection of the most popular. What's YOUR favourite?

## No build

Building structures is a key part of the gameplay in Fortnite, and while it can be a lot of fun, it can also become repetitive. By playing the no-build mode, you can experience a different kind of gameplay that requires a different set of skills. This can help keep the game feeling fresh – but it has other benefits too!

No-build Battle Royale is great fun in its own right, but is also a valuable training tool to help improve your combat. Because you're not allowed to build structures to protect yourself, you will quickly learn to improve your aim and remain mobile in combat — skills that will also come in extremely handy if you return to the normal Battle Royale mode. You'll also need to be more strategic about where you move and when you engage in combat, making smarter decisions about when to engage an opponent and when to stay out of sight.

# Creative

This is a sandbox mode that allows you to create your own maps, game modes, and experiences. It's a great way to let your imagination run riot and create something truly unique. With so many different tools and options available, there is no limit to what you can design in Creative— and there are thousands of talented map-makers out there creating games for you in this mode too, so you can take inspiration from them!

The only limit is your own imagination. You can build your own Battle Royale map, sure, but that's just the beginning. You might want to build a racetrack, or a parkour course to race round. You can design custom games to play with your friends – some people have even used creative mode to make their own music videos and short films!

No matter what you are interested in, there is something for you to do in Creative. It is a great way to have fun with your friends, learn new skills, and express your creativity.

# Ranked

This is where things get serious! Ranked is the complete opposite to the casual fun of Creative or Party Royale! In this mode (again, playing in solos, duos, trios or squads) you compete to earn points – an in-game ranking system. You're awarded points based on how high you finish AND how many eliminations you get. The more points you get, the more you can climb through the rankings with the aim of reaching Unreal status. Climb high enough up the rankings and you can enter the biggest tournaments for cash prizes, but be warned - the skill level is sky-high and you will need to put in a lot of practice before you start to climb your way to the top!

# Party Royale

Grab a big bowl of crisps and your favourite drink, stick your headset on, put your feet up and get ready for some chill time! Party Royale is the social scene of Fortnite – there's no combat, just fun and friendship. Throughout the year, Fortnite plays host to all manner of special events too – from movies to concerts, with special parties often thrown for events like the Superbowl. If you want to spend an evening catching up with your buddies – or you're looking to make new friends with a shared interest – then Party Royale is the answer!

CONNECTING

Experiment with building piece edits... There are lots of valid shapes.

# Save The World

If you like a bit of history, Save The World is actually what Fortnite was intended to be. Yup, that's right, the whole Battle Royale mode wasn't even included to start with! Save The World focuses on a storm closing in around the world (sound familiar?) that turns people into zombies. You play the role of a storm survivor and you must build structures and use weapons to repel wave after wave of zombie attacks.

This is a paid-for extra, and is quite a fun blast for a while. However, it's not hard to see why Chapter 1 Season 1 (which only contained this mode) failed to really capture the imagination of the gaming public. It was only when Battle Royale was launched in Chapter 1 Season 2 that the numbers started to snowball and Epic realised that they had a hit on their hands after all!

# Zone Wars

Some Fortnite gamers love the whole experience – dropping in, harvesting materials, building their armoury, and enjoying as the action slowly heats up as all the players are pushed together by the storm. Others find the first part of the game boring, and live for the crazy action of those last few storm circles.

If that's you, then you'll love zone wars-themed games. They basically replicate the endgame, with up to 16 players dropped into a very small circle. You'll usually start with a predefined set of weapons right in front of you and a set level of materials, and then it's time to unleash hell! As well as being great for a quick Fortnite fix, zone wars games are a great way to practice your techniques and strategies for handling those closing battles. If you find that you're regularly making the top ten but not kicking on to secure the Victory Royale, then this could be the training tool you've been looking for!

# Deathrun

Deathrun games challenge you to navigate increasingly difficult obstacles without dying. Most deathrun games include an element of speed – think Temple Run with a big dollop of Fortnite! It's a fun and challenging game mode that lets you put your weapons away for once, and because you're mainly completing with yourself to improve on the time or the distance you survived for, the levels can be enjoyable regardless of your skill level.

Another big advantage to playing deathrun games is that it can really help your building, editing and jumping skills, as many games of this type require you to build or jump your way through the gaps – you can then take your newly honed skills back into Battle Royale to become an even more formidable foe!

# Box Fights

Box fights are pretty insane, but can be great fun (and help improve your building too! They are basically battles on very small maps – sometimes 1v1 but sometimes involving up to 16 players - and the idea is to outbuild your opponent so you can take the high ground and outshoot your opponent. They're especially good fun when played with a friend so you can take each other on for bragging rights – perhaps head online with a friend and the winner gets to choose the loser's skin for your next duos match!

BOX PVP

A Jump
B Boost
LB Handbrake
LT Air Roll (Hold)
RB Camera Toggle
X Exit (Hold)

# Driving

Some gamers avoid the vehicles in Fortnite completely, but for others they are the best bit! If you like nothing more than leaping into a fast car or onto a trail bike and tearing it up round the Island, then you should check out some of the thousands of various different driving games that are available. Most involve racing pre-determined vehicles round a track but there are other games too – variations on Rocket League, games where you have to destroy each other's cars – you name it, if it involves a vehicle, someone has made a Fortnite game that involves it!

# Prop Hunt

If you love a good game of hide and seek, then prop hunt games are the Fortnite mode you've been looking for! It's good wholesome fun that means you can put your weapons away for a little bit and engage in some good clean fun!

Prop Hunt sees players split into two team – hunters and props. The props team transform into everyday items and then have to hide around the map – most prop hunt games have a specific theme, and the props available to disguise yourself as will match that theme. Once the props are hidden, the hunters have to find out where their opponents have hidden before the clock runs out! If it sounds simple that's because it is – though it's great fun to play with friends in a group chat and tease each other with 'warmer' and 'colder' clues...

# Wordsearch

Can you find all the words in our list, hidden in the wordsearch?
Words can run left to right, top to bottom, or diagonally!

```
M V D S T C C R E A T I V E K
H T I Q A U F N T J Y L O O T
I S E C L V R V D O O I Q I C
B L S P T V E T L T I N W Q A
E U N H I O B T L Z Q C E U K
A R I N H C R U H I K V C S F
U P P L F N G Y C E N T N E Y
T G E O D S S A R K W G H A B
O S R Q O I F K M O S O B H T
M G H K H W N A D E Y S R V V
A S L O O A K G V B S A F L J
T T M A T E R I A L S C L C D
I O Z I D G N Z W L J Q Y E N
C R U V L R U E U K I I M V C
J M E P H O W N W B F E J L E
```

| | | | |
|---|---|---|---|
| Save the world | Vbucks | Slurp | Jonesy |
| Victory royale | Building | Shotgun | Materials |
| Creative | Turtling | Sniper | Loot |
| Epic games | Storm | Automatic | |

Answers on page 78.

# Crossword challenge

Can you complete our tricky crossword? All the answers are referenced somewhere inside this book!

## Across

2. A weapon that is most effective at close range (7)
4. The name of the company that publishes Fortnite (4)
7. A method of rewarding you for progressing through the game, which can be spent on skins and more (6,5)
8. A short name for the bullets you need for your weapons (4)
9. The in-game currency (1,5)
10. An upgrade you can buy that allows you to unlock skins and more as you increase your ranking (6,4)

## Down

1. The name of one of the default skins (6)
2. The name of the original Fortnite game mode (4,3,5)
3. The item you use to drop in from the Battle Bus (6)
5. Winning a game will give you one of these (7,6)
6. A famous Australian streamer with his own skin (9)
7. The name given to the part of your outfit you wear on your back (4,5)
11. The magical liquid that can heal and replenish shields when consumed (5)

# Answers

## Wordsearch answers

```
M V D S T C C R E A T I V E K
H T I Q A U F N T J Y L O O T
I S E C L V R V D O O I Q I C
B L S P T V E T L T I N W Q A
E U N H I O B T L Z Q C E U K
A R I N H C R U H I K V C S F
U P P L F N G Y C E N T N E Y
T G E O D S S A R K W G H A B
O S R Q O I F K M O S O B H T
M G H K H W N A D E Y S R V V
A S L O O A K G V B S A F L J
T M A T E R I A L S C L C D
I O Z I D G N Z W L J Q Y E N
C R U V L R U E U K I I M V C
J M E P H O W N W B F E J L E
```

## Crossword answers

1. JONESY
2. SHOTGUN / SAVETHEWORLD
3. GLIDER
4. EPIC
5. VICTORYROYALE
6. LAZARBEAM
7. BATTLESTARS / BACKSLING
8. AMMO
9. VBUCKS
10. BATTLEPASS
11. SLURP